INTRODUCTION

This pamphlet is a handbook of negotiation tactics. None of the tactics are original, but none of them can be attributed exclusively to some other author. All have been in use for millennia and children learn some of them by the time they are five, as any parent can testify. Therefore, instead of the clutter of footnotes, there is a bibliography, incomplete and quickly outdated as all bibliographies must be, but useful as a starting point for the reader who recognizes the pervasiveness of negotiations in modern life, and their usefulness in settling disputes among families and nations, and at every level between. My major debt is to Chester Karrass (1974), although any comparison will reveal many differences. Most obvious of these, Karrass provides very brief treatments—in one instance only two words—of 200 tactics (many of which I regard as different names for the same thing), while I have attempted longer discussions of only 48.

With the decline of support staff and the rise of word-processing, professors no longer have secretaries to thank for typing manuscripts. Instead, my thanks are to Dr. William Dickerson, Renaissance scholar, college roommate, and printer, who made several important corrections and suggestions, without becoming responsible for the errors that remain.

Tactics provide the means by which negotiators attempt to

1

achieve their goals. A useful analogy is to football, where the goal is to outscore the other team, and the tactics by which this is attempted include a dazzling variety of passes such as the bomb, fly, post, buttonhook, square in, square out, slant in, flare, roll out, screen and play action. All of these tactics work some of the time; none work all of the time. Success depends on skillful execution, appropriate timing and luck— which in that overused phrase, a team makes for itself. The stronger, more skilled team wins most of the time, but upsets do occur.

Unlike football, there is nothing arcane about negotiating tactics. The revelation will not be the tactics, but in realizing how familiar most of them are. Familiarity is not the same as mastery. There is a vast difference in the way a professional and a high school football team execute plays and a similar difference in the way experienced and inexperienced negotiators use the tactics.

Nor is there anything very new about negotiating tactics or the purposes to which they are put. There is much talk in the 1980s about negotiation as an innovation to reduce the financial and psychic costs of divorce. But John Romer (1984) has provided the details of just such a negotiation conducted in Egypt about 1200 BC in which price and quality of cloth figure into the alimony. Sumerian merchants trading barley and lapis lazuli 4000 years ago would recognize the tactics of modern diplomats negotiating nuclear arms limitation treaties. Teenagers wishing to stay out late would recognize the tactics of union leaders in a labor negotiation. Legislators resolving differences in senate and house versions of a bill would recognize the tactics of medieval Polish parents negotiating a dowry. Whatever the place, whatever the time, whatever the subject, negotiators have tried to reach agreement using the same basic tactics.

Tactics that have been found useful for so long under so many circumstances do not depend on trickery or the stupidity of opponents, as some mistakenly think. It is much more useful to think of them as ways by which negotiators explore the possible existence of, and move toward, a mutually acceptable beneficial settlement.

Despite the universality of negotiating tactics, there is no agreement on what they are called or how many there are. For example, "linkage," "log rolling" or "tie-ins" could be treated as one tactic or as three. Combining them risks obscuring subtle differences, while discussing them separately risks repetition and unnecessary proliferation. I have chosen the first risk. Despite the arbitrary nature of the names for each tactic, I discuss them in alphabetical order. Some say there must be a more useful arrangement—but have not suggested one. The problem is that the tactics are useful at every phase of a negotiation, and almost any one can be used in conjunction with, or in opposition to, almost any other.

TACTICS

1. ACCEPTANCE TIME. Negotiators often begin with over-optimistic goals or unrealistic hopes. One function of a protracted negotiation is to give all parties time to adjust to and accept more realistic ideas of what can be achieved.

Acceptance time is used to convince opponents that their aspirations are absurdly optimistic and totally unrealistic, so must be reduced if a settlement is to be reached. Therefore, negotiators seldom make early offers bluntly. They are more likely to explain their reasoning first. This implies that the offer is serious, even if it is not. Alternatively, negotiators may be apologetic or wheedling before making their offer. Listening, opponents gradually realize that the offer will not be what had been hoped, and this softens the blow when it does come. Skillfully done, opponents will even feel relief that the offer is not as bad as the explanation made them expect!

Allowing time between making a proposal and trying to close the agreement can save having to make further concessions, because it allows opponents to to conclude (rightly or wrongly) that no more concessions will be made. A negotiator wanting to exploit this psychological characteristic will minimize the amount of explanation preceding an offer, but extend the explanation following it.

2. AGENDA. Agendas can be explicit and agreed to in

writing, which is common in union contracts negotiations, government procurements or international treaties. Or they can be implicit and unwritten, which is common in sales negotiations, family disputes, plea bargaining, legislative conferences, and most sales negotiations. Negotiators can seek advantage on the basis of the completeness, order, or phrasing of the agenda.

Negotiators can strive for an agenda that addresses items on which they are strong or with which they are most concerned, but omits those that weaken their position. A simple example is avoidance by a car salesman of the subject of taxes, license and preparation fees, tacking them on once the deal is reached. The buyer can counter by making offers that allow for the amount that will be added at the end, in effect allowing for a final agenda item. Negotiators must protect themselves by identifying all issues in advance and making sure each will be included in the agenda. If all parties do so, a fair, complete agenda will emerge. If not, the agenda is likely to give the more astute an advantage.

Advantage also can be sought in the order in which items are addressed because they may not be equally important to all parties. Price is the most important item in most sales, but the buyer may be concerned most with down and monthly payments and delivery date; and the seller with interest income, risk of default, and eliminating slower selling items from inventory. Other aspects of the sale, such as options, warranties, and delivery date may vary widely in their importance among parties. Two factors must be considered in seeking this advantage.

The first factor is whether to address important issues early or late. Simply because energy declines with time, there is a tendency to deal more quickly and less thoroughly with each successive item. There also is a tendency not to let the time invested go to waste by deadlocking on later agenda items, regardless of importance. Therefore, negotiators in strong positions usually prefer to deal with important issues first, while those in weak positions usually prefer to deal with them last. If strength varies issue by issue instead of overall, negotiators will try to deal early with those on which they are strongest.

The second factor in considering the most advantageous order for agenda items is the amount of concession possible on each. A negotiator may prefer to deal first with items on which large concessions are possible, requesting compensating concessions on later ones in the interest of a "fair" overall deal. This may work if the latter items also are relatively unimportant to the opponent. But it also may backfire if the large concessions on early items suggest that they can be obtained on *all* items.

Finally, one side can seek advantage by phrasing agenda items in terms of their own goals, placing the opponents on the defensive from the start. A classic example of this is the agenda proposed by the Chinese during the Korean War truce talks. The first item proposed was:

> Establishment of the 38th parallel as the military demarcation line between both sides, and establishment of a demilitarized zone, as basic consideration for the cessation of hostilities in Korea (Joy, 1970).

The 38th parallel had been the prewar boundary between North and South Korea, and the battleline at the time crossed it diagonally, leaving the North Koreans in possession of a small area south of the parallel, while the United Nations held a much larger area north of it.

It is perfectly legitimate to seek any possible advantage in setting the agenda. It is equally legitimate to resist an opponent seeking to gain such an advantage. This sometimes requires persistence. It took ten plenary sessions to achieve neutral phrasing on the Korean War truce talks. The first item finally read:

> Fixing a military demarcation line between both sides so as to establish a demilitarized zone as a basic condition for the cessation of hostilities in Korea (Joy, 1970).

3. AMBIGUITY.   Our culture and our schools teach us to strive for clarity and precision in speaking and writing. We try to anticipate every possible future situation, and to provide for it in advance. When this makes both parties feel protected, it makes agreement easier. But, it sometimes makes reaching agreement harder, because it focuses attention on what can go wrong, gives as much importance to minor matters and unlikely events as to essential ones, or even creates differences that did not exist to begin with.

Ambiguity has a place in negotiations. During talks, ambiguous statements can give the appearance of sympathy for opponents' needs without actually making concessions, so can improve the bargaining climate and make eventual agreement more likely. Opponents about to walk out can be kept at the bargaining table by an ambiguous statement. If it is recognized as such, they will tend to request clarification, which keeps the talks going. If it is not recognized as such, they will tend to interpret it in their favor, which also encourages them to keep talking.

Ambiguity permits reaching agreement on some issues while delaying settlement of others. The War of 1812 settled the U.S.-Canadian border from the Atlantic to the Great Lakes, but left it ambiguous to the west, where neither side had yet penetrated sufficiently to understand or stake out its claims and interests.

Ambiguity permits negotiators on all sides to claim that they have have wrung concessions from opponents and have preserved vital principles. The agreement leading to the release of the American hostages by Iran allowed Iran to claim victory over "the Great Satan," while the U.S. could argue that they had confessed to nothing. Thus, both sides could satisfy their own constituents that the result was satisfactory. An agreement can succeed with both clear and ambiguous language if all parties are clear as to what each can do, must do, and must not do.

Negotiations tend to begin ambiguously partly because it is easier to clarify an ambiguous statement than to equivocate once a precise statement has been made. There are many ways to create ambiguity. People have difficulty separating facts from assumptions, and difficulty determining which assumptions are appropriate in a particular circumstance. This is very much the case when such intrinsically uncertain matters as bad debts, depreciation, future value, indirect costs and return on investment must be considered. Numbers may appear precise but often are based on assumptions. People have difficulty separating facts from assumptions and difficulty dealing with ambiguity.

Numbers provide an excellent means of providing whatever degree of ambiguity or clarity is desired. Dollars are clear, compound interest on unpaid balances less so, and agreements providing adjustments for inflation even less so. Mixing fractions and decimals together is confusing. Probabilities — particularly joint probabilities — are difficult to interpret (should you carry your umbrella if there is a 60% chance of rain and a 25% chance that you will lose it whether or not it rains?). People often accept averages as explanations whether they apply or not. Decimals have a way of making things look more precise than they may be, and are easy to obtain, without fudging, by subjecting numbers to calculations involving division.

4. ANGER.   Anger is common in negotiations. Some negotiators lose their temper according to plan (and therefore have to be good actors). One version of the famous incident in which Nikita Khruschev banged a shoe on the table at the United Nations is that it was an extra carried in his brief case. Anger can be used to show that a particular issue is more important than the opponents might otherwise think, or to hint that a deadlock may be in the offing unless some progress is made. Sometimes it will convince opponents that they have pushed things as far as possible. Sometimes it will make opponents feel guilty or ashamed; either way anger can lead to concessions by the opponents.

Real anger provides a dangerous opportunity. A person who gets angry (or begins to cry, or otherwise loses control) often is easily fooled or will make errors or concessions out of shame once calmed down; if the opponents also get angry, or treat real anger as a negotiating ploy, the negotiations may break down permanently. It takes considerable experience to remain cool in the face of anger. In most cases, it is better to wait till things calm down, or recess until they do, or try to calm opponents down.

5. AUTHORITY.   Negotiators usually have limits on their authority to conclude an agreement. The Constitutional requirement for Senate approval of all treaties limits the authority of the President. Purchasing agents are given dollar limits and sales personnel discount limits beyond which they must consult higher authority. Some negotiations involve components for which negotiators have different limits. For example, a purchase may involve negotiation of down payment size, number of payments, trade-in allowance, delivery time and costs. A negotiator may have separate limits on each component. It is important to understand how much authority your opponents have on each component of the deal on which you are working.

Limited authority may be an intentional tactic to keep opponents off balance, tire them out, or facilitate retreat from previous concessions. One way to accomplish these purposes is to pass the opponent on to successively higher ranking people. Each time, the concessions made by the opponent are treated as the starting point of the discussion, while those made by one's own agent are denied, ignored or repudiated as beyond the agent's authority.

When the tactic is expected (e.g., in buying a car, where it is almost certain) the initial negotiations should be viewed as opportunities for such tactics as building acceptance time, collecting information, or establishing an agenda. Generally, it is vital to hold sufficient major concessions to force the final authority into the open and to maintain negotiating room. Ways to smoke out this individual vary with circumstances but include threatening deadlock, having one's superior call the opponent's superior, obtaining the intercession of a third party, or bringing in specialists such as lawyers, financial analysts, and technicians.

As you reach each higher level of authority, it is vital to prevent opponents summarizing your concessions without summarizing those made by their subordinate. Sometimes a written record, agreed to and signed by all parties, is made before continuing negotiations at higher levels. This is usual in formal negotiations that involve long-term relationships, such as that between unions and employers, or in international relations (where they are known as *aides memoire*). They would be unusual in consumer purchases—but this might give them tremendous impact!

Another approach is to seize the initiative and state the opponents' concessions without stating one's own. A third is to bring in your own higher ranking authority—whether that means your boss or your spouse. Finally, and particularly if the authority of the lower ranking agents to make the offers they did is denied, opponents can be accused of failing to bargain in good faith.

An entirely different use of authority tactics is to delay making a decision that may be regretted later. In this case, the individuals will not change but the negotiations will be protracted and will involve frequent caucuses with a superior. A variation on this is a superior who is sick, on vacation or does not even really exist. Well-timed demands to negotiate with the person who has final authority will lead to that individual or, if it is a ploy, to an announcement that the current negotiator has been given greater authority.

6. BACK CHANNELS. Back channels refer to secret discussions outside the formal negotiating process. They are used to overcome deadlock, in very sensitive circumstances or as a face saving device. But, their very secrecy deprives the back channel negotiators of needed technical advice to make the best possible bargains. They have been much used by American presidents: Colonel House served Wilson, Harry Hopkins served Roosevelt, McGeorge Bundy served Kennedy and Kissinger served Nixon in this capacity. They play a major role in overcoming deadlocks in union negotiations.

7. BAD GUY/GOOD GUY.   This tactic is familiar to anyone who has ever seen a police movie. One negotiator, the bad guy, uses threats, anger, unreasonable demands and other harsh tactics to soften up opponents. The other negotiator, is kind, gentle and understanding, blaming all difficulties on the bad guy while seeking to obtain concessions and agreement.

The tactic has many variations. The bad guy may confront the opponent, or may be a superior who is consulted whenever the opponent senses that the only alternative is a major concession. The bad guy may or may not really exist. The bad guy may not be very bad at all, but simply all business, serious, and plain-spoken, while the good guy is always smoothing matters over with a joke or a story. The bad guy could be a collective, such as a board of directors that must ratify any agreement. The bad guy may not be human at all, but a company policy or a law you or the opponent claims to have no authority to change or dare not violate.

The bad guy/good guy technique can be countered by protesting either to the opponents or to their superiors, by bringing in your own bad guy or by laughingly comparing the effort to a bad police movie to demonstrate that it is not going to have any effect. If the bad guy is not a person but a rule or policy, you often can suggest reasons why you warrant an exception. If it is a law, its applicability to the situation can be refuted or questioned.

8. BARGAINING CLIMATE. The relationship among negotiators can be professional, trustful, and courteous— or it can be the opposite. The first usually is both more pleasant and more efficient. The relationship can be formal or informal, though which is best depends on the situation and the individuals involved.

A reputation for keeping both the letter and the spirit of agreements improves the bargaining climate. Learning and using the names of opponents, courtesy, kindness, food and drink are traditional ways to improve the negotiating climate, although combined with jet lag they can be fatal to a negotiator's judgment and are often used to advantage by hosts in international negotiations. Small favors improve the climate, but large ones become bribes, which are illegal in some cultures, expected in others and a source of confusion and difficulty when representatives of cultures with different views on the subject negotiate.

The climate deteriorates if a negotiator suspects, even wrongly, the good faith of opponents, or is subjected to personal attacks, *ad hominems,* or one upmanship. When faced with such treatment, a single warning that you will walk out if they continue, then doing so if there is no improvement, usually is an effective way of handling such situations. In some circumstances, the warning will gain force if it includes a threat to explain the reasons for any walkout to the opponents' superior. The tactic will of course backfire if the real intent of the abuse is to get the opponent to break off the negotiation.

Humor can change the climate either way. It can relieve tensions, or be used to build a common bond through light-hearted jokes about common problems. But, it also can offend an opponent. If not used carefully, particularly in inter-cultural situations, humor aimed at relieving tensions can have the opposite effect.

Climate also is affected by expectations of how long the bargaining relationship will last. The tradition of courtesy to representatives of a country no matter how outrageous its current behavior stems from the essentially permanent relations among nations. A car salesman is likely to treat a buyer of a family car, unlikely ever to be seen again, quite differently than a fleet buyer who makes large annual purchases.

9. BARGAINING STRENGTH (or bargaining power). Many factors real, assumed and perceived, affect bargaining strength. Negotiators must assess their own real strengths and weaknesses. They must assess those of their opponents as accurately as possible and be careful of the assumptions made in the process. They must think about ways to change their opponents' perceptions of relative strength and they must consider the impact of current actions on long-term bargaining strength with the opponent.

Bargaining strength is the ability to influence others. Unless each party has *some* source of power, unconditional surrender is more likely than negotiation. Total powerlessness is rare, despite the difficulty and creativity that may be required to identify what little strength a party has. Despite France's total military defeat in 1940, the possibility that its fleet would sail to Britain and that an exile government would emerge in its colonies was sufficient to convince the Germans to preserve the appearance of continued independence. The Germans ultimately did take over Vichy France — but not till the Allies destroyed or controlled what was left of the French fleet and DeGaulle had created an effective exile government.

Bargaining strength has two forms and many sources. The two forms are positive, the ability to get things done, and negative, the ability to prevent things getting done. The latter is particularly important within modern bureaucratic organizations.

Strike funds and ICBMs are forms of strength, because they convey the possibility of causing harm if agreement is not reached. But, the most important kinds of power are intangible. Image is power: Carter was a weak president partly because he seemed uncomfortable with and unlikely to use power; Reagan was a strong president partly because he seemed comfortable with and likely to use power.

Likableness is power. Reagan survived Irangate, and Nixon was destroyed by Watergate, partly because of likableness or the lack of it. Ruthlessness is power. Lyndon Johnson bullied opponents. Hitler and Stalin killed them.

Money and people are power. In twentieth century American politics, the Republicans have tended to have the former, and the Democrats the latter. Strike negotiations have sometimes turned on the cash flow of the business compared with the size of the union strike fund, or on the availability to the company of nonunion labor compared with the availability to strikers of temporary jobs.

Legitimacy and precedent are power. Proposals gain power based on such sources of power as published price lists, legal requirements, and consistency with past practices or industry standards. Presidential proposals have more power than ambassadorial ones; compulsory arbitrators have more power than mediators. Published prices, or limited authority to make concessions, legitimate the power of a salesman to resist demands for concessions so increase bargaining strength.

Credibility and trust are power. Capacity to influence is enhanced by a reputation for candor, honesty, integrity, and commitment to promises—or threats—made.

Knowledge is an important source of power. Among the forms it takes are analytical, circumstantial, creative, legal, substantive, technical, strategic or tactical. This pamphlet deals only with the last.

Alternatives and flexibility are power. The more ways a negotiator has to achieve a goal, the less threatened the negotiator is by the prospect of deadlock with an opponent. A negotiator needing transportation who will consider bus, bicycle, motorcycle, and car has more flexibility than one limited to a car; a car buyer willing to consider several makes has more flexibility than one who will consider only one, and a car buyer in a city with many dealers has more flexibility than one in a small town with only one dealer (who also is a customer of the buyer).

Time is power. Knowing an opponent's deadline gives a negotiator who has a later one considerable power. But, it is easy hand to overplay. The trick is to prevent the opponent walking out until it is too late to make a deal with a third party.

Bargaining strength increases with willingness to risk failure, which depends in turn on what is at stake, how the odds of success and failure are assessed, and personality.

Understanding opponents is a source of strength. Factors

such as conduct, reputation, past bargaining behavior, needs, costs, benefits, and risk proneness should be considered. The tendency to exaggerate the strength of opponents, and to assume that they have the same risk factors as oneself, or even are as risk prone or risk averse as oneself, must be guarded against. Understanding translates into an ability to make proposals that move toward agreement.

External events can change the relative bargaining strength of the parties during the negotiation. Instances include changing interest rates or rising domestic opposition to a war. Negotiators who feel time is on their side naturally will attempt to draw negotiations out, while those who feel the opposite may make concessions to hasten agreement. Alternatively, they may wait for circumstances to change, may take steps to change circumstances themselves, or to strengthen the resolve of their own side.

Negotiators with little bargaining strength often rely on trying to improve the bargaining climate, confusing the issue, hot buttons, linkage, or salami slicing. They may try to increase their power by changing the agenda. Those with great bargaining strength can make particularly effective use of hot buttons, take it or leave it, and threats.

10. BEST AND FINAL OFFER. Negotiators sometimes are called upon (particularly in a competitive situation or in dealing with the U.S. government) after negotiations have been going on for some time to make their "best and final offer." This implies that the offer will be assessed and either accepted or rejected without further negotiating. In practice, recipients are likely to try further negotiation anyway to make sure it really is "best and final."

Knowing this, negotiators sometimes allow for one or two

final small concessions beyond their "best" and "final" offer. A reputation for negotiable "final" offers being undesirable, the alternative is to to react to efforts to obtain further concessions by pointing out that the offer is a good faith response to the request (implying bad faith on the part of the opponent in asking for further concessions), meant just what the term implies, and that there will not be any further concessions. That is, take it or leave it. Calculated anger often stresses the points. It may be necessary to deadlock once in a while so that future best and final offers will be taken seriously.

Negotiators sometimes initiate the process themselves by identifying an offer as "best and final" (or, even more strongly, as take it or leave it). One reason for doing so is to retain or seize the initiative by preventing an opponent making their own best and final offer before you do.

The recipient of an unrequested best and final or take it leave it offer has several options. One is to take it seriously, and to accept it (if it is within the recipient's settlement range). A second is deadlock. A third is to treat it as a concession and the basis for further negotiation. Still other approaches are to change the specifications and request a new offer, to change the subject and keep on talking, to ignore it, to respond to an earlier proposal as if it still were on the table, to request a recess, to explain what deadlock will cost the opponent in the short- and long-term, feign anger, or bring in higher authority. It is vital to have sufficient tools to keep negotiations going in the face of "finality."

11. BETTER THAN THAT. Opponents often can get significant concessions simply by saying "You have got to do a lot better than that." Unskilled or tired negotiators often assume what kind of improvement is required (e.g., price) and make unthinking concessions. It is much wiser to find out what is wrong with the current offer and why, so that an offer can be made that has some chance of being accepted. The objection that the competition is offering a better deal is a dual opportunity. You may learn something new about the opponents, useful in the current negotiation or in a future one. Or you may be able to demonstrate ways in which your offer is better despite differences.

12. BLUFFING AND LYING.   Bluffing is more common than, and less frowned upon, than lying, but both occur so must be guarded against. A negotiator can bluff or lie either by commission, omission, or interpretation. Deliberate errors are a time-tested means of lying to gain advantage. The base by which percentages are multiplied (e.g. from net to gross sales or vice-versa) can be altered. A seller can imply that a reduced price applies to a higher quality of goods than is being discussed. Dates can be changed, "mistakes" made in arithmetic. Words can be added, omitted or changed. Price can be inflated by adding the same item in more than once. Or, in a classic seller's trick, some item can be "forgotten" until the "error" is caught by a supervisor before approving the final deal, then added back into the "agreed" price.

Bluffs and lies are common in low-trust conditions but are more effective in high trust situations. They are much less damaging to the overall negotiation in low- than in high-trust conditions. That is, the rewards of bluffing and lying are directly proportional and the risks inversely proportional to the level of trust. Because level of trust and credibility do not preclude such tactics, the negotiator must always guard against them.

13. BOTTOM LINE. The "bottom line" refers to the final total benefits and costs of a deal. Negotiators often try to distract opponents from the bottom line by discussing prices on an item-by-item basis (come down a penny to $.49 a pound and you have a deal), percentages (come down a quarter point and I'll agree to the mortgage) or the size of monthly payments. In doing so, they obscure the total cost (a penny a pound on a million pounds is $10,000, a quarter point on a mortgage is likely to cost thousands; low monthly payments may mean that the debt outlasts the useful life of the product and doubles its price). Negotiators must be careful to determine both immediate and total costs of an offer.

14. CAUCUS. A caucus is a private meeting among the negotiators on one side. A caucus may be no more than a brief whispered conversation without leaving the negotiation table, or may involve a private meeting of a negotiating team in a separate room (which in some circumstances may have been bugged by opponents). Time for a caucus can be requested at any time, but a longer negotiation also provides natural opportunities such as meal breaks.

A common reason for requesting a caucus is to review a new proposal from opponents, or one with unexpected components. A caucus requested for this reason creates the obligation, or at the very least the expectation, that a response to the proposal will be made when the negotiations resume. Caucuses can be requested for other reasons as well, such as reviewing progress on each objective, assessing the opponents' objectives, revising tactics, consulting with higher authority or pretending to do so, talking with the opponents' competitors, sorting out confusion within the team or breaking the momentum of the opponents (much as is done in some sports).

Obviously enough, when the opponents are making concessions or appear to be under pressure, it is unwise to request a caucus that will allow them to accomplish any of these same purposes. Generally a request by the opponents for a caucus is respected. It is possible to oppose a caucus request or, less harshly, to try to delay it or limit its length, perhaps by pointing to a *deadline*. But, doing so risks having one's own caucus requests refused or limited in future, or deterioration of the bargaining climate or long-term relationships among the parties.

15. CLOSING. Six important closing techniques, some with variants, are described below.

The first technique is based on asking questions. The simplest version simply is to ask for agreement to your current offer. Another is to ask a series of questions that can be answered with a simple yes or no, but selected so they always will be answered yes. An easy way to get into the sequence is to review what has been accomplished, or to review your understanding of opponents' needs. Whenever a "no" is encountered, the question must be revised until the opponent agrees with it. Once the opponent has said "yes" to each agenda item, shift the questions to formalities, such as who will be signing.

Another version is to keep asking the opponents what objection they have to your offer. Dispose of them one at a time and end each time with "if there are no more objections I assume we have an agreement." When the opponents run out of objections, it is difficult for them to do anything but close.

Still another version is to answer a question with a

question. If a buyer ask "If I bought this computer, would you throw in a box of floppy disks?" the seller might answer, "If I could do that, would you be prepared to buy today?" This works *if* the buyer has made a demand the seller can meet.

The second technique is to summarize everything so far agreed, emphasizing the concessions already made to (not by) the opponents, pointing to the advantages and justice of agreeing to the current proposal, and suggesting that the advantages of immediate agreement outweigh the disadvantages of continued haggling. A common mistake is to belittle the remaining issues, as opponents can then ask you to give up what you have admitted is unimportant.

A variation is to summarize all points in favor of agreement and all points against it, this time pointing out that the weight is with immediate settlement rather than continued haggling. If the points actually are listed in two columns on a piece of paper, this is known as the "Ben Franklin close," based on the way Franklin claimed to make decisions.

If tried on you, you can agree completely (closing the deal), disagree completely (risking deadlock) or suggest that the summary is generally acceptable then specify the items on which you still require improvement.

The third technique is to try to close a negotiation by giving opponents a choice among two or more proposals, each feasible to the offeror. One version focuses on product. For example, a salesman might ask whether the consumer wants the red sports car with the stereo system for $19,000 or the yellow sedan with the air conditioning for $18,000. This has the advantage of offering the opponent a choice among possible agreements, rather than between agreement and continued negotiation. The technique is particularly appropriate when the settlement range is understood but the relative importance of the opponents' needs are not. Obviously, if you are the recipient of such a choice, you should not feel constrained by them. Given the previous choices, you might request that a stereo system be added to the yellow sedan with the air conditioning for a total price of $17,500.

Another version focuses on price. For example, a luggage salesman trying to make a $200 sale might say that some people require the features on the $295 model (a figure *about* 25% above target), some need the luxury model for $450 (a figure *at least* 50% above target), while some will be satisfied with the standard model for $200. The salesman will then ask which of the three most meets the buyer's needs. Given the $200 answer, the salesman will then emphasize that the $200 model meets the buyer's needs. Given the $295 or $450 answer, the salesman than can emphasize that the buyer's needs can be met for much less than planned, building good will that may lead to future sales.

The fourth technique is to try to close a negotiation by offering a concession contingent on final agreement. One form of this, used when objectives are not equally important to each party, is to offer agreement and a concession on one or more issues in exchange for agreement and a concession by the opponent on the remaining unsettled issues. The simplest, and the most simplistic, is to suggest "splitting the difference." If this is tried on you, you have three choices. You can accept the split, accept the idea of a split but reject the assumption that it be 50-50 and suggest some other split such as 75-25 in your favor, or you can treat it as a concession by the opponents. To do so, calculate just what "split the difference" comes out to, treat the figure as just another offer, and make your own counteroffer.

The fifth technique, relatively common in international negotiations, is to try to delay resolution of some issues to a future negotiation. This can succeed when one or more of three circumstances exist. First, neither side wishes to endanger progress already made. Second, the unresolved issues have long-range rather than current importance. Third, one side regards the issues as non-negotiable. In the first circumstance, the delay is mutually advantageous so most easily achieved. In the second circumstance, parties with different expectations for the future hope that delay will enhance chances of achieving their own objectives on the issue. In the third circumstance, agreement to delay consideration effectively acknowledges that the issue really is negotiable, while any agreement not to take the issue up may effectively concede to the side that claims the issue is not negotiable. As both of these represent a concession, though by opposite sides, compensation may be sought elsewhere.

The sixth technique is to make absolutely clear that no more concessions are forthcoming. There are four versions, varying primarily in tone. Best and final offers puts the stress on the advantages of reaching agreement. Threats put the stress on the negative consequences of failing to reach an agreement. Take it or leave it offers fall between these two in tone. Finally, the remaining difference can often be trivialized. For example, a remaining difference of $3000 on an office machine likely to be kept for three years can be translated into a weekly ($19.23), daily ($3.85) or even hourly ($.48) cost and the value of the machine compared to prevailing wages.

If you are on the receiving end of one of these techniques, you have several choices. You might change the subject and keep talking, ignore it and keep negotiating on the basis of an earlier proposal, or request a caucus to gain time. If the difference is being trivialized, you can ask for a trivial change in your favor (say, reducing the cost to $.47 an hour, saving $62.40.

All six techniques are possible. If one fails, another can be attempted. The techniques have been listed as nearly as possible in increasing forcefulness and in declining number of options they leave to opponents. Experience suggests that it is advantageous to use the least forceful possible closing. But, it also is important to have sufficient mastery of the closes to have an alternative ready when a particular one fails. Finally, if a close fails, the negotiator must choose between trying another close immediately or resuming bargaing before trying to close again.

16. CONCESSION RATE. Negotiators expect to make several concessions from their first position. This should be planned for. I suggest setting four objectives for each issue. Start with your Deadlock position. One of the best suggestions for choosing it is Fisher and Ury's (1981) concept of the Best alternative to a negotiated agreement [BATNA]. Basically, it requires that you assess the cost of alternatives to reaching agreement. For example, if you don't buy a house, what are all the costs (including lost tax deductions, etc.) of continuing to rent. Next is your Realistic position—the one which, based on all you can learn about your opponent, the situation, and yourself, is your best estimate of what you can achieve. Next is your Optimistic position—the position you might achieve if your opponents need to settle quickly or have not assessed the situation accurately—and the point at which you will stop making concessions until you get to the opposing negotiator with the authority to make a final agreement. Finally, set your First position— your opening bid. Taken together, the four positions have their own easy-to remember acronym, FORD.

It is neither necessary nor wise to match your opponents' concessions in value or number, and naive to expect them to match yours. Negotiators try to prevent opponents guessing accurately—or even think they have guessed accurately—just what their settlement range is.

Concessions can be made at a regular rate (the same amount each time) or an irregular one. Too large an initial concession may lead the opponents to think they have a pigeon, while delaying any concession for too long may suggest lack of good faith. A regular rate, or even worse, a larger and larger concession each time, makes it difficult to signal opponents that you are reaching the point at which no agreement is possible and suggests to them that patience will be rewarded. Due to exhaustion, lack of confidence, fear of deadlines or lack of skill, negotiators often make large concessions toward the end of a negotiation, giving away all they have gained. Thus, patience can bring advantages even from apparently tough opponents.

A substantial concession followed by progressively smaller ones suggests a willingness to compromise and signals opponents that the limit is being reached. An irregular pattern (sometimes substantial, sometimes trivial, sometimes moderate, sometimes no concession) suggests willingness to compromise, but makes it more difficult for opponents to ascertain the point at which the negotiator will deadlock.

There is a psychological element to the completion of every deal. Those made too quickly always leave people with the uneasy feeling that they might have been cheated, or might have made a better deal with someone else. People tend to feel best about those they have worked hard to achieve. For this reason, too, concessions must not come too frequently nor any deal concluded too quickly.

17. CONFUSING THE ISSUE (or Snow Job). Negotiators might try to confuse the issue by illogical statements, red herrings, overwhelming complicated technical or financial details, statistics, or possible alternative deals, then discussing them all at once in no sensible order. The tactic can be used in the early stages to test the opponents' preparation, in the middle stages to lure them into mistakes, or in the latter stages in hope that tired opponents will prefer agreement to thinking through the implications of all the new concepts. It can be used to divert attention from a question you don't want to answer. The technique can be countered by insisting on adherence to the agenda, insisting that each variation be taken up in turn, refusing to talk about the variations, or insisting on a full explanation of each variation. If the variations were introduced primarily to confuse, they probably have no substance and will be withdrawn quickly.

Detecting and countering illogical arguments, or determining whether statistics should be believed or not, are complex studies well beyond the scope of this little pamphlet. Much has been written on both. I suggest Fisher's *Historians' Fallacies* and Katzer's *Evaluating Information*.

18. DEADLINES. The negotiator under the greatest time pressure is at a serious disadvantage. Negotiators therefore usually try to conceal their own deadlines while trying to learn the opponents'.

Deadlines are useful in other ways. Deadlines can provide important protection. For example, failing to put an expiration on an offer to sell your house makes it impossible to make an offer to a second possible buyer without risking a lawsuit by the first one. Deadlines can encourage an opponent to settle. For example, telling buyers that the price will go up at the end of the month or that on-time delivery requires a firm order by the end of the week give opponents reasons to act promptly (Notice that these last deadlines do not place opponents in take it or leave it positions—both permit continued negotiation without loss of face).

If you are given a deadline by your opponents, you can take it seriously, ignore it, or try to negotiate a new one. The first course usually concedes bargaining strength to opponents. The second gains bargaining strength if the opponents are bluffing, but makes deadlock likely if they are not. The third reduces the opponents' bargaining strength to the extent that it rested on the original deadline.

19. DEADLOCK.   Deadlock ends a negotiation; the *possibility* of deadlock is a tactic. When faced with a deadlock, unwilling to accept the terms offered, and desirous of reaching a settlement, negotiators can request a caucus to discuss the offer or otherwise delay proceedings. They can ask for clarification of the terms offered and lead from there into a review of the entire negotiation, so that both parties keep talking. They can point out the implications to the other party of failing to reach agreement. They can ignore the offer or change the subject, or shift the discussion from the specifics of an agreement to reaching an agreement on broad principles and common interests, or at the opposite end of the scale turn to minor issues or even procedural matters as where to continue the discussion. They can ask hypothetical questions about the impact of possible changes in the offer. Above all, when faced with an undesired deadlock, keep talking or make sure it is possible to do so after a break.

Alternatively, seek explanations to facilitate reopening negotiations later. Techniques for reopening deadlocked negotiations include agreeing to talk off the record for a while, backchannels, starting over by varying the nature of the discussion (e.g., changing the specifications or payment methods) or replacing the negotiators who deadlocked with higher ranking negotiators. The side that initiated such a deadlock often derives an advantage, as the opponents often are willing to make significant concessions to keep the negotiations going. In this case, credit for softening up opponents, rather than condemnation for failing where others succeeded, often should be given to the deadlocker.

Because deadlock often causes frustration, anger and a sense of failure, it is a powerful way to test an opponents' resolve, but loses credibility if overused (like the boy who cried wolf). If done too abruptly, it will become final because the opponent will have no time to implement tactics such as those just described. If done too slowly, or with too much dependence on such cliches as slowly putting papers into a briefcase preparatory to walking out, it may be perceived as a bluff and turned on its maker.

Deadlock is the appropriate outcome of a negotiation in which no settlement range exists. It is important not to confuse deadlock as a tactical device with the deadlock price discussed in conjunction with the preparation phase in the preceding chapter.

Deadlock is the appropriate outcome of a negotiation if the highest price the buyer will pay is below the lowest price the seller will accept. Not all negotiations should end in agreement. Negotiators probably should be (but seldom are) rewarded for avoiding bad agreements.

20. DELAY. Negotiators sometimes want to slow down the pace of a negotiation. They may believe that the opponents' can be forced up against their deadline, believe that their own bargaining strength is likely to increase shortly, need time to think, or be waiting for additional information. Delays can be for a few seconds or a few months. Delays can be of specific or uncertain duration.

Negotiations can be delayed by requesting a caucus or by confusing the issue. They may be delayed by telling a joke, going to the bathroom, or asking for a coffee or meal break. They can be delayed by a detailed exploration of an issue — and the choice of a false, trivial, peripheral, or key issue can be significant. They can be delayed by presenting background information (sometimes beginning with Genesis), discussing precedents or regulations, or reading lengthy documents into the record. Another classic technique is insisting on delaying a final decision until a committee of specialists — usually financial, technical or legal — investigates specified matters. The makeup of the committee can itself be the subject of almost endless negotiation. There are ample devices to delay a negotiation.

21. EMPATHY. Empathy is a matter of imagining oneself in the opponent's place. It is a device for improving the bargaining climate by demonstrating that the opponents' problems are understood. It is useful in conditions of high tension or low trust because it demonstrates willingness to understand the opponents position.

In the negotiating context, it can be developed, then reinforced, by "empathic listening," as developed by the psychologist Carl Rogers. The technique involves presenting one's own position only after you have restated the ideas and feelings of opponents to their satisfaction, then requiring them to extend the same courtesy to you. This is intended to demonstrate that you are willing to make the effort required to understand their concerns and needs, which makes it difficult for them to remain angry with you or to continue feeling that you are being unfair to them. It also is intended to encourage opponents to understand that your concerns and needs are legitimate as well. And it is intended to improve listening and reduce the tendency of opponents to interrupt one another, as it becomes impossible to restate a position you have not listened to carefully.

22. FACE SAVING. Skilled negotiators try to make it easy for opponents to make concessions. In general they provide opponents with a way to change a previous offer without *appearing* to make a concession at all, or give them a good reason for retreating from the previous position. Some devices that permit face-saving are (1) reviewing the assumptions on which offers are based, (2) raising new issues that have not yet been taken into account, (3) trading one kind of concession (e.g., delivery date) for another (e.g., price), (4) stating needs and demands firmly but prices ambiguously avoids premature commitment and facilitates making concessions.

23. GOOD FAITH. Negotiators sometimes try to soften opponents' positions by accusing them of bargaining in bad faith. But opponents cannot be proven to be bargaining in bad faith simply because they have not made a concession as readily as hoped (see the discussion of concession rates), or because an offer is completely unrealistic (see the discussion of offers). They cannot be proven to be bargaining in bad faith simply because they interpret facts differently or provide only partial answers to questions (see the discussions of ambiguity, bluffing, and questions). Multi-cultural negotiations—which include negotiations involving different socio-economic groups or even different professions in a single culture as well as international ones—may have quite different concepts of what is and is not ethical. Even illegal tactics, such as bait and switch, may be difficult to distinguish from similar but legal variants, in this case the Sibylline books. Virtually every charge put forth as evidence of bad faith by opponents may be no more than tough negotiators using perfectly legitimate tactics. Bad faith is an easy accusation to make, but a difficult one to prove.

Accusing opponents of bad faith when they view their actions simply as good tactics can undermine the bargaining climate. But, negotiators who fail to point out tactics that are offensive take the risk of appearing to be too weak to protect their own interests, a situation likely to lead to deadlock if false and to disadvantageous agreements if true.

24. HAGGLING. Haggling consists of alternating, converging, offers by each party until agreement is (or is not) reached. Often it is closer to ritual than to bargaining. Haggling is the main form of bargaining in oriental bazaars, street markets and swap meets but is common also in settling small remaining differences during the closing phase of major negotiations.

Haggling is a simple process, with a settlement very close to the point half way between the first offers of each party being likely, *if* that point is within the settlement range. Thus, it involves a lot of verbal fencing to maneuver the opponent into making the first offer. Then it is easy to subtract the first offer from the price they hope to settle on, then add (if selling) or subtract (if buying) to arrive at one's own first offer.

The disadvantage of having made the first offer can be overcome by refusing further concessions or making very small ones till the mid-point between the parties is acceptable, by the Sibylline Books tactic, or by threatening deadlock. I have found it useful when shopping for souvenirs in countries where I have no idea what the price of an item should be, and I have been maneuvered into the first offer, to laughing loudly and suggesting the local equivalent of a penny and start to leave. This usually smokes out a legitimate first offer from the merchant. Incidentally, five star hotel and airport duty free shops are a simple way to get a feel for the high end of the local price structure.

25. HOT BUTTON. Negotiators like to find and push their opponents' "hot button," the underlying need that will make almost any deal irresistible. Some people want to save money, some to save time, some want to save—or avoid—work. Some want to be in the know, some want to be in style. Some want prestige, some want power, some want security. If a buyer is worried most about getting a production line going quickly, the seller should emphasize immediate shipment and installation of the needed equipment. If the buyer's profits are down, the seller should emphasize that the new equipment will cut production costs. If the buyer is frustrated by rapid obsolescence, the seller can offer liberal trade-ins or inexpensive upgrading to newer versions. Identification of hot buttons is best done early in a negotiation; pushing them is best done as you begin trying to close.

It is of course impossible to list all the possible hot buttons, and even if such a list were available, it would be difficult to run through such a list to determine which ones applied to a particular opponent. Several efforts have been made to develop general taxonomies. Maslow's (1954) is the best known. His hierarchy runs from basic to higher needs as follows: Physiological; Safety and security; Love and belonging; Esteem; Self-actualization; Intellectual; Esthetic.

Maslow argues that people strive to meet these needs progressively. The idea then is to identify which need an opponent is striving at, and to pitch your offer in those terms. In practice, it may be easier to identify the level opponents already have achieved, and to assume they are striving for the next level, than to identify where they are at directly.

The major categories of Maslow's hierarchy may prove too general to be of much use in a negotiation. A "quick and dirty" approach is to rate opponents subjectively as high or low on formality and initiative and to orient questions during the exploration period to testing and refining the probable dominant needs suggested:

Initiative	Formality	Probable Dominant Needs
high	low	personal (e.g., honor, ego gratification)
high	high	professional (e.g., power, quality)

| low | low | interpersonal (e.g, recognition, love) |
| low | high | security (e.g., financial, emotional) |

The implication of both formulations is that proposals should be shaped to meet needs. The further implication of Maslow's hierarchy is that any difference in needs between two new negotiators gives greater bargaining strength to the one seeking higher needs. This provides an abstract explanation of the advantage of international terrorists, as governments are concerned with saving lives, the lowest possible need, while the real motive of the terrorists usually is publicity for their cause, a form of self-actualization.

26. IGNORANCE. Negotiators usually feel a need to demonstrate mastery of their subject, but feigning ignorance is a good way to obtain useful explanations, gain time to think and, pushed to the extreme, drive opponents to real and thus exploitable anger. Tactical ignorance can be countered by confusing the issues, information, questions and answers or asking opponents to be less ambiguous in their questions so you can answer them properly.

Ignorance as a tactic should not be confused with real ignorance. The negotiator who has not prepared adequately is at the mercy of the opponent. The ignorant usually make very bad deals and often are unaware of the fact.

27. INFORMATION. Information can be sought, withheld or given. If received from an opponent, facts should be verified and assumptions should be tested before they are taken too seriously. Information from opponents may have errors of commission or omission. Testing can be done through independent sources, or through tactics such as ignorance, objections, or questions.

Negotiators must be careful not to give up bargaining strength by letting opponents know of time, financial or other pressures they are under. Therefore, negotiators usually try to give opponents as little information as possible. But, they cannot expect opponents to make useful offers without information about their needs. As both sides face the same dilemma, negotiators exchange rather than give away information.

Sometimes reversing the norm can work. A full disclosure of the problems a negotiator faces sometimes can win the sympathy of opponents or (more likely and more usefully) involve the opponents in finding a creative and mutually advantageous way to meet a negotiator's needs. The tactic is common among professional negotiators who represent absent clients.

A perverse way of limiting the opponents' information is to overwhelm them in a blizzard of detail that exceeds the ability of anyone to analyze and interpret. The information should be as voluminous, technical, trivial, and poorly organized as possible. It can contain errors and contradictions. Put forth in the guise of being open and cooperative it even can improve the bargaining climate. Subsequent questions are answered by telling the opponents that the answers are in the materials they have been given. This often results in confused opponents poking about randomly for a short time and not asking any more questions. If faced with this tactic, ask for the specific references that answer each of your questions and then for a recess to review the materials.

Another approach to providing information is to call on an expert — or someone who appears to be one. Experts have great credibility but can be challenged by your own, preferably of greater age, self-confidence, number of degrees, publications, reputation, and ability. Other possibilities are broadening the discussion to the point that the knowledge of the expert appears too limited to be useful, or narrowing it to the point where the knowledge of the expert appears abstract, academic, and irrelevant.

Information need not be obtained directly from opponents. Libraries, public records, information services (e.g., Dun and Bradstreet, Consumer Reports), newspapers, professional societies, government studies, annual reports provide vast amounts of information on almost any topic. It is just a matter of allowing sufficient time and money to find, collect, organize and assess it.

28. LINKAGE (Tie ins or Log-rolling).   Negotiators can try to get what they need on one issue by offering a concession on another issue. The success of the technique depends on issues having differential importance to each side, so that each can make an unimportant concession to get one that is important. It depends also on how an agenda that allows exploring all issues then making proposals, rather than exploring and settling each issue independently in turn.

Linkage can involve closely related issues such as down payment, installments and interest rates. But they need not be related at all: prestige may be important to one party and ideology to the other. Nor need they be equal in number: precedent and tradition may be important to one party and appearances to the other. The most satisfactory and creative solutions often are the ones that achieve the most unexpected linkages.

If all acceptable outcomes on all issues were known, it would be possible to plot all the possible linkages. The economist Vilfredo Pareto has demonstrated that these will fall within a curve which has come to be called the Pareto Optimal Frontier. Any settlement that does not lie on this curve can be improved upon by both parties. But, without perfect information about both parties, it is impossible to tell precisely where the curve lies, so it is of relatively little practical value in real world negotiations.

29. NONVERBAL COMMUNICATION (or Body Language). Communication involves both receiving and sendng signals, and nonverbal communication must be considered from both viewpoints.

As a way of understanding opponents, nonverbal communication probably is highly overrated. It is likely to be misinterpreted because a gesture may have no meaning (consciously or otherwise), may vary in meaning among cultures, social classes or individuals, or because opponents are intentionally sending false nonverbal signals. Despite this, fidgeting, folding arms or reviewing notes probably indicate inattention or disinterest and a change from whatever is being done at the moment should be considered.

As a way of influencing opponents, nonverbal communication is even more overrated. One active technique that may have some value in making opponents more comfortable with you is imitating them in mood, posture, speech patterns (rate, tone, volume, phrases, imagery) and breathing patterns—unless they think you are mocking or manipulating them. Personal characteristics such as stuttering, or gestures such as crossed arms that may indicate opposition should *not* be imitated.

30. OBJECTIONS.   Negotiators raise objections to reduce opponents' aspirations and to expose weaknesses, offset weaknesses in their own position or signal their own needs. They can object to almost every aspect of their opponents' position. They can object to the accuracy or relevancy of the opponents' facts, or the interpretation or conclusion given to them. They can object to apparent lack of good faith, unnecessary delay or the setting. They can object to any of the terms of a proposed agreement, to shortcomings of the product or service or to the financial arrangements. Some objections are planned in advance, but some of these (such as the lack of leg room in the back seat of a car) have become such cliches as to have no real force.

Negotiators must deal with as well as make objections. First, they must be sure to understand the objection. Some are ambiguous, intentionally or not. "My people won't like that" could refer to price, to the time it will take to learn to use new equipment, to changes in procedures that a new system will require, or color. "People" could refer to superiors, subordinates, colleagues, stock holders, or customers. Answering by reducing selling price may be making an unnecessary concession that will not satisfy the objection. An objection must be understood before responding to it.

Objections can be refuted. This requires identifying assumptions (the inflation rate will remain high), interpretation (inflation is important), errors of commission (the inflation rate has been overstated), errors of omission (no allowance has been made for inflation) or conclusion (inflation was allowed for twice, once on raw materials and once on total costs).

Some objections are aimed at a negotiator's aspirations. Sometimes these objections can be ignored or glossed over with a joke. Sometimes weaknesses can be turned into an advantage (this sometimes is called turning lemons into lemonade). For example, if an opponent complains of an obsolete component, point out its incredible reliability. If opponents raise a large number of objections, surprise that they did not go to a competitor can be expressed. Opponents then have to explain why they want to deal with you, taking the sting out of their own objections in the process.

Some objections signal the opponents' needs. These objections should be investigated rather than refuted. Generally, this requires expressing understanding of the concern but the need for more information to be able to respond to it. Empathic listening and careful questions generally are the best approach.

The practical difficulty in dealing with objections is selecting among the different approaches. Trying to understand an objection raised to lower aspirations, or trying to refute one raised to signal needs is going to do a negotiator more harm than good. This reemphasizes the importance of understanding an objection before responding to it.

31. ONE TEXT PROCEDURE. The one text procedure involves continuing modification of a draft agreement by all parties to develop successively more acceptable drafts until all parties accept the current one as acceptable.

The one-text procedure is useful in multi-party negotiations, or where a board or policy group, perhaps representing very different viewpoints, must announce a position. Generally, one person will suggest a statement for all to endorse, someone will object to an implication, someone will suggest new phrasing to accommodate the difficulty and after one or more rounds agreement will be reached. Additional objections will be dealt with similarly. This tends to minimizes continual rehashing of the same arguments without any progress made toward agreement. The one-text procedure often is more efficient than other ways of reaching agreement in multi-issue, multi-party negotiations.

The one-text procedure also is useful in high-tension low-trust negotiations. A draft agreement, clearly labeled as such, can be submitted by one party for suggestions by the other party. If attention can be shifted from unfocused argument to quibbling over specific language, both parties will have less to get angry about, and will also sense that agreement is beginning to emerge.

The one-text procedure can also be conducted by mail or by intermediary. Because people have a chance to review and revise their writing, because most people are careful about what they put in writing, because recipients of unnecessarily antagonistic letters can cool down before responding, because most people tend to be brief and to the point in letters, the one-text procedure carried out by correspondence can be very useful in cases of extreme tension. It may be useful too where distance makes it difficult for people actually to get together. People who write better than they speak under pressure may prefer it, and can be useful as well if a detailed record of the negotiation is desired. Modern communications using computers and fax machines make it fast and efficient.

32. PERSEVERANCE. Negotiations completed in haste often are regretted at leisure. Perseverance requires toughness and insensitivity. Practically speaking, it involves outwaiting opponents, endlessly repeating the same proposal without any concessions, by infrequent or minute concessions, or by other delaying tactics. Carried to the extreme it risks deadlock, so is best employed when opponents need an agreement and can only get it in one place.

The reasons for doing so include wearing opponents down, lowering their expectations, leading them to make concessions or eliminate red herrings in hope of progress eliminate red herrings. It can insure that all problems are discussed and that all needs are understood before settlements are reached. It allows creative solutions to emerge.

Negotiators who are deprived of sleep or suffering from jet lag, who are suffering from too little or too much food or drink, or under stress for any reason are less likely to persist and more likely to make mistakes. As the negotiation grows in importance, more and more attention should be paid to the creature comforts of the negotiators, and to making sure that they eat at normal times and get sufficient rest.

33. PERSUASION. Opponents make agreements to meet their own needs, not yours. The only reason they may show interest in your needs is so they can push your *hot buttons* to their own advantage. Persuasion tactics are not used in negotiation to convince opponents that your needs are their needs. Just the opposite. They are aimed at convincing opponents that an agreement is in their own interest—that it meets their needs.

It seldom works to define a problem as you see it, then the logical solution as you see it. The opponents may not accept your formulation. They may think some of the factors you mention are trivial or that you have misinterpreted them. They may think you have omitted some important considerations. What is logical to you is may not be logical to them.

When opponents show resistance to your ideas, the natural thing to do is to try to convince them that you are correct and they are wrong. But, it may be more effective to switch than fight—to change tactics if the issue must be settled immediately and to change topics if it can be settled later. It sometimes is useful to imitate the major perceptual mode of the opponent, which can be identified from the the phrases used (I hear you, I can see that, that looks difficult, tell me more about that, that feels right; how does that sound?, do you see what I mean? does that look any better?, what can you tell me about that?, how does that feel?).

In classical terms, as worked out by Greek orators, persuasion begins with opening words to win attention and good will, an explanation of how the problem developed, a direct statement of the case and an outline of how evidence will be presented. This is followed by the body of the argument, divided into three parts including (1) confirmation of one's own case by presenting facts, reasons, statistics, opinions, testimony, reports, examples, analogies and other evidence, (2) refutation of opposing views as untrue, illogical, contradictory, ambiguous, dishonest or absurd, and (3) alternatives to any legitimate points that favor the opponents. Finally, the argument is concluded with a summary and a final appeal for support (Berke, 1985). Such long complex presentations are rare in modern argument or negotiation. But the method can be effective even if developed across many shorter statements.

34. PRECEDENT. Negotiators sometimes say that they

could not possibly meet opponents' demands because they would have to make the same concession to everyone else. It is a powerful tactic because it obviously is difficult to determine whether the negotiators really would treat the concessions as precedents in future deals. A variant is for negotiators to claim that they have a government contract that precludes their giving a better deal to anyone else.

If faced with this tactic, four counter tactics are possible. The first is a series of questions, first confirming that the opponents are serious about precedents then asking how they keep track of them, and finally asking for a list of all precedents affecting you. If done too quickly, the opponent is likely to see the purpose, but if drawn out, the opponent will be placed in the position of bargaining in bad faith if the request is not met when the trap finally is sprung.

The second counter tactic is to argue that the current deal is sufficiently unique that it is not covered by the precedent clause. The third is to make sure the opponent actually is offering terms as good as they gave the government, then to ask for evidence of just what those terms are. The fourth is to use linkage to obtain concessions elsewhere (perhaps citing a few examples of government overpayment such as the recently notorious $150 hammers, or reaching back to the 1930s when the government bought a hundred thousand or so feedbags for the 50 or so horses remaining in the army).

35. PRECONDITIONS. One or more opponents may decline to negotiate at all until preconditions have been met. Sometimes these represent legitimate concerns, for example when they involve mutual rules for dealing with any media interest in a negotiation. But, when one side seems overanxious to negotiate, opponents may try to obtain concessions on real issues as a precondition for negotiating. Or, preconditions may be attempts to gain small psychological advantages leading to an advantageous bargaining climate or setting.

Typical preconditions involve the agenda, negotiating conditions, setting, status or rank of negotiators, order of speaking, use of experts, symbols of authority, use of tape recorders, release of information to the media and responsibility for record-keeping. It usually is advantageous to have the latter responsibility, and it often can be gained simply by including a secretary on your team.

36. PROPOSALS. Ostensibly, proposals represent the terms currently available to opponents. But, they can serve other purposes, such as conveying determination or trying to reduce the opponents' aspirations. Proposals can be made merely to prevent deadlock by giving parties something to talk about. They may have nothing to do with actual hopes, but be made to hold the constituency a negotiator serves, or to influence public opinion and thus alter bargaining strength.

Negotiators can accomplish these purposes by tone and phrasing. Describing a proposal as a suggestion, a demand, or an ultimatum will have quite different effects. Proposals can be sufficiently attractive to generate interest but sufficiently ambiguous to encourage questions. Ambiguity makes them easier to withdraw, replace or change. Proposals aimed at clients or the public often contain popular principles but few specifics. For these reasons, proposals cannot be taken at face value. In interpreting a proposal, all these possibilities must be considered, but so too must be the possibilities that the opponents are not well prepared, are unskilled, or may not have read the same books about negotiating.

Proposals can be ignored, laughed off, rejected, questioned or accepted. Explanations, justifications, modifications, or time to consider them can be requested. Counterproposals can be made, which are ambiguous or clear, or described as suggestions, demands or ultimatums.

37. QUESTIONS AND ANSWERS. There are three general ways to ask questions that move a negotiation toward resolution of issues. The first is aimed at getting action. Examples are asking if everyone is ready to move to the next issue on the agenda as a means to keep things moving or asking who will be signing the agreement as a means of gaining commitment to closing the negotiation at the current terms.

The second is aimed at getting information from opponents. This is the most common, the most important and the most obvious purpose for questions. Questions allow negotiators to test assumptions; to discover additional facts or information; to clarify, verify and analyze statements by opponents. Questions provide a way to challenge facts and assumptions without direct attack, and to test the opponents absolute and relative commitment to each of their objectives and thus to identify their priorities.

The third is aimed at giving information or signalling. These questions often are rhetorical. Often, the second and third purposes are combined. Thus, asking how far a piece of property is from an airport provides the seller with a much more accurate idea of what the buyer needs than simply asking where the property is located (the question also is ambiguous—it is not clear if the buyer wants property that is near or far). Negotiators sometimes forget these purposes or get carried away with attempts to one up opponents by their superior intelligence or wit, usually to the detriment of the bargaining climate.

Questions can be general or specific: the answers usually will have similar scope. General questions (such as the airport example above) are useful for identifying needs. Specific questions provide and obtain more precise information. Questions usually become more specific as a negotiation continues. Specific questions asked early may miss the mark and reveal information prematurely. General questions asked late risk opening new issues, suggest inattention to earlier answers, and are less likely to move the negotiation toward a close.

Questions can be phrased to give opponents varying latitude in answering. A question such as "What kind of home are you looking for?" gives buyers complete freedom to respond: or instance, desired size, location, or style. A question such as "Are you ready to look at the kitchen now??" invites very few responses: yes, no, not quite yet. A leading question, consisting of a leading statement ending with an interrogative, such as "This is a very pretty room, isn't it?" almost forces a yes answer. Rhetorical questions such as "Doesn't everyone know that falling interest rates mean houses are selling very fast these days?" require no answer and are intended to provide rather than obtain information.

Questions usually are asked singly, but can be asked in succession, with or without giving the opponent a chance to answer them or even answering them oneself. This technique maintains control and can be effective in leading an opponent to accept your conclusion.

When it comes to answering questions, negotiators are

48

cursed with having been students, imbued over the years with trying to answer clearly and completely, afraid to look stupid. Politicians provide a better model. They know which questions to answer, which questions to avoid. They know when to be clear, when to be ambiguous. They answer parts of some questions, or avoid giving more details by repeating previous answers. They answer questions that were not asked, rephrase the question the way they wish it had been asked then answer that question, give a reason for not answering it, or simply say they can't answer the question. Negotiators should watch the news conferences of skilled politicians to learn how to answer questions.

38. RAISIN PICKING. Just as children sometimes "pick the raisins out of the cake," negotiators sometimes attempt to assemble what they need from the best deal on each needed component. They begin by obtaining detailed bids from competitors, then follow one of two approaches.

The first is to review the bids and buy each component from the supplier who offers it most cheaply. Many shoppers use this approach, going from store to store to get each item they need at the most favorable price. But, unless they are careful or know what they are doing, they may lose more in time and travel costs than they gain by the effort. Worse, sometimes components from several sources do not function well together.

A second approach is to review the bids and to use the lowest bid on each component regardless of source as the basis for a counteroffer to one or more bidders. This approach avoids the disadvantages of the second approach and puts the bidders on the defensive, as they must explain why their prices are higher on some items. But, it gives the bidders more latitude for reply.

39. RED HERRING (Strawman or Throwaway). Negotiators sometimes raise issues or take positions in which they
have no interest, defend these red herrings at length, and
finally try to surrender them in exchange for real concessions.
A car buyer can easily begin negotiations for a car that
includes one or two perfectly normal options — expensive
hubcaps and a luggage rack, for example — of no real interest.
Well into the negotiation the buyer can complain that the
requested price still is too steep and give up the hubcaps. The
trick of course is to request a reduction in price greater than
that of the option being sacrificed. Later, the luggage rack
can be given up to signal that the buyer is unlikely to make
any more concessions.

40. REVERSE AUCTION. The reverse auction may be
useful in buying a complicated but poorly understood product. Buyers of computer systems may not understand what
the issues are, what questions should be asked or what options are open to them. In a reverse auction, sellers are asked
for bids knowing who they are bidding against. This encourages each seller to offer the best possible price and to
explain the advantages of their own and the disadvantages
of the competitors' product. The information gained then is
used to revise the specifications before inviting revised bids.

One approach when faced with a reverse auction is to try
to be the last to bid, and to learn as much as possible about
the competing bids. If this is not permitted, ask for an
opportunity to respond to the opponents' bids. A second
possibility that strikes more directly at the motivation behind
many reverse auctions is to demonstrate to the opponent a

willingness to understand and meet their needs. Once understood, the idea is to to demonstrate that the special characteristics of one's own product are precisely the ones the buyer most needs, while its weaknesses (which cannot be hidden because the competition will point them out) do not affect the buyers' purposes.

41. SALAMI SLICING (or Nibbling, Nickeling and Diming, Taking One Step at a Time).   Salami slicing, from the way butchers can slice meat to fill a sandwich as cheaply as possible, refers to efforts to get one small, painless concession after another, until they add up to big ones.

Salami slicing is one way to make progress under conditions of low trust, in which case not only should the equested concessions be small, but the agenda should begin with issues of low importance to the opponent. The goal is as much to improve the bargaining climate as it is to settle issues. Salami tactics also are useful when an opponent is known to be under deadline pressure. The progress being made makes it unlikely the opponent will turn to a competitor, while the slow pace may force the opponents to make major concessions as they run out of time. Salami tactics provide a means of making it difficult to establish linkage among issues.

A variant of salami slicing (nibbling) often used by buyers is threatening to back out of a deal at the last moment unless some small extra is thrown in. The classic case is a man asking for a free necktie with the suit, shoes and shirts he has just bought, after the tailor has taken the measurements but before the buyer has written his check. Other examples include last minute requests for extra services, free advice, improved delivery schedules, free alterations, improved packaging or extra manuals. Sellers nibble as well, by suggesting small accessories as a sales slip is being prepared.

Many regard nibbling as unethical. The usual devices for defeating it include published prices, ignoring nibbles, politely explaining that it cannot be done, treating it as an old joke everyone uses, including the price of the nibble in the original price, or co-opting the buyer. The last means no more than anticipating the nibble and suggesting the item or service as part of the deal before the buyer does. It is very difficult to tell a salesman that no tie is necessary and a few minutes later to threaten to throw up the whole deal if a tie is not provided free. But, above all, it must be remembered that the buyer too has a lot of time and effort invested in the deal, and is unlikely to go through the whole process again for so small a benefit.

42. SETTING.   Negotiations have taken places on golf courses, in restaurants, in railway cars and in every other conceivable setting. Venue can have an important effect on outcomes. The four basic possibilities are the negotiators' territory, the opponents' territory, alternating between the two, or neutral territory. The advantages and disadvantages of each possibility should be weighed, and the choice never be left exclusively to opponents. The best setting is the one that maximizes control of the bargaining process, and what is best can vary from one phase of the negotiation to another.

Negotiating on home territory makes it possible to put on demonstrations to impress opponents, provides access to needed staff and information, and better control of schedule and atmosphere. Traditionally, negotiations occur in the territory of the stronger party, so negotiating at home provides possible psychological advantages. Opponents on their own territory gain these same advantages.

Negotiating on the opponents' territory makes it possible to collect information you do not have, to obtain delays by claiming the need to refer questions to higher authority, or to walk out — something hard to do from one's own office. Opponents on one's own territory gain these same advantages.

Alternating between territories of opponents is a common compromise. Advantages still can be gained, usually by conducting the early stages on the opponents' territory, and the later stages on one's own territory. But this is not an invariable rule and thought should be given to the various possibilities raised in the particular situation. Negotiating on neutral territory generally takes place under conditions of low trust or high conflict. One major advantage is that interruptions are virtually eliminated.

One aspect of the setting that gets considerable attention is seating arrangements. Opponents usually sit along opposite sides of a rectangular table, or across a desk from one another, a setting that stresses the adversarial nature of the relationship. The usual approach to downplaying differences among parties is a round table. The famous dispute over table shape in connection with the Vietnamese peace talks was not trivial. The United States insisted that the talks were among themselves, the South Vietnamese government and the North Vietnamese while the North Vietnamese insisted that the parties consisted of themselves, an independent Viet Cong revolution, and the United States including their South Vietnamese lackeys. A table shape had to be found that made it clear that there were three sides but left ambiguous just who was included on each.

Some negotiators try to manipulate the environment even

further. During the Korean War truce talks, the Chinese tried devices such as chairs with different heights so opponents had to look up at them, forcing opponents to look into the glare of lights, making their own flags larger and higher than the UN flags, and sitting on the side of the room that, in Asia, was reserved for the victors. Admiral Rickover used to seat junior officers for hour long interviews in a chair, one leg of which had been shortened by an inch. Efforts of this sort should be resisted as a failure to bargain in good faith.

Luxury can awe or soften some opponents but can backfire if the opponents think of it as an overhead cost that must be factored into every deal. The reverse strategy of pure, spartan efficiency can work as well. The effort to strike the right tone also can include great attention to detail, in the selection of the diplomas and photos displayed or the temperature, lighting and ventilation in the room. Your office conveys impressions to visitors that you are sloppy or neat, lazy or industrious, inefficient or efficient, weak or powerful, dull or interesting, harassed or in control, incompetent or competent.

43. SIBYLLINE BOOKS. The oracle Sibyl offered nine books of prophecies to King Tarquin. Tarquin offered a lower price than asked, which Sibyl answered by burning three of the books and offering the remaining six at the same price. Tarquin protested at paying the price for nine books when only six remained and Sibyl burned three more. Fearing that Sibyl would destroy the remaining three, Tarquin paid the price asked for all nine to get them (Bullfinch's Mythology, XXXII).

Negotiators expect opponents to begin with extreme positions then make concessions until an agreement is reached.

But it is possible to follow Sibyl's practice and raise the offer instead. The usual method is not through destruction but to begin with an attractive offer on a low-cost model, then demonstrate that all sorts of extras (or a higher priced model) are needed. A variant is to point to conditions (e.g., interest rates) that have changed during the course of negotiations that require an adjustment in the original offer. Another is to invalidate a previous concession on the basis of an opponent's failure to meet conditions attached to it.

The technique is a useful counter to salami slicing. Taking back a small concession diverts the opponents' energy from getting small concessions from you to restoring concessions they already had counted on. Used this way, it is a signal that the opponent had better start worrying more about averting deadlock and closing the deal. As it risks charges of not bargaining in good faith, justifications are important when using the tactic.

This tactic can degenerate into the unethical and often illegal "bait and switch" tactics in which buyers are told that the "limited quantities" of the (non-existent) product offered at the special price are sold out but that the deluxe model still is available at the regular price. Buyers can bait and switch too, by sealing a deal with a token deposit, waiting till the seller is up against a deadline, then threatening to back out unless the price is reduced. Buyers may have legal recourse against "bait and switch," but sellers protect themselves best by large deposits.

44. SIGNALS (or Trial Balloons).   A signal or trial balloon is a hint of a direction or topic that one side would like to pursue at a particular time. A signal might indicate willingness to make concessions if the opponents are willing to reciprocate. Such a signal can suggest the areas in which concessions are offered, it can suggest the areas in which concessions are desired, it can do both or it can be general. A signal might indicate a desire to move on to another topic, or to another phase in the bargaining process — from exploration to bargaining, or from bargaining to closing.

A signal can show up as a condition, a qualification, a direct suggestion or an action. Calling something impossible is not a signal, calling it unlikely or difficult may be. Calling some elements of a proposal nonnegotiable (e.g., price) signals that those not mentioned (e.g., quality) may be. Asking a question (e.g., what delivery date does that price guarantee) signals the buyer's desire to explore a particular way to change the price offered). Stating the rationale on which price is based (e.g., our price is based on orders of 1000 per week for a year) suggests that price is affected by the size of the order. Assembling papers preparatory to leaving to signal an approaching deadlock has become a negotiating cliche. The possibilities are endless.

Signals usually are ambiguous (and therefore must sometimes be repeated several times before they are recognized). For example, the buyer just mentioned who was asking about delivery date may be trying to determine what if anything early delivery will cost or may be trying to determine if waiting will earn a price break. Therefore, a signal should lead to questions rather than offers until it is clear exactly what the opponent needs or wants. The seller might answer the question about delivery date and ask if that is acceptable, might counter with a question as to when the items are needed, might suggest that orders are filled as received, or might suggest that waiting until the items can be combined with other shipments to the same would permit a reduction in delivery costs. Again, the possibilities are endless and of course depend on the specific situation. But, it is important to respond in some way so that the opponents know the signal has been received!

A signal avoids commitment. It avoids the possibility of offering a concession to an opponent that is accepted without reciprocation. Because a signal avoids commitment, the discussion that follows can be hypothetical. Because a discussion is hypothetical, it is easier to abandon an unproductive line without loss of face. But, if it proves productive, it permits negotiators to offer specific concessions with conditions attached that opponents have in effect already agreed were acceptable.

Signals between China and the United States from 1969 to 1971 led to resumption of diplomatic relations. It began when two American yachtsmen capsized and were rescued by the Chinese. The signal was the absence of the usual anti-American propaganda. The United States answered by allowing American tourists to import up to $100 of Chinese goods. The Chinese released the yachtsmen, and the Americans eliminated the $100 ceiling on Chinese goods bought by tourists. The Chinese then gave permission for U.S. subsidiaries to sell goods to China. All of this involved improved relations but no commitment. But then China pardoned a bishop serving a 20-year sentence for spying—an official act of clemency. The U.S. responded with permission for U.S. companies to sell components to China. The famous invitation to the American ping pong team came next, followed by permission for U.S. companies to sell nonstrategic goods to China.

Less interesting, less subtle, but much more common, are signals based on selection or treatment of envoys. Reagan signalled a desire for better relations with Greece by appointing an old friend of Papandreo as ambassador. Displeasure can be signalled by keeping a new ambassador waiting to present credentials (thus denying him the ability to function officially), or reducing the level of access. For example, Britain did not receive the new Polish ambassador for weeks to show disapproval of martial law in Poland in 1981, and Robert Kennedy made clear to the French ambassador that he no longer was welcome at the White House after DeGaulle vetoed English admission to the Common Market. Ambassadors are not without responses. They can send inappropriately junior diplomats to functions, stay away entirely, or walk out ostentatiously in the middle of someone's speech—behavior frequently seen at the United Nations.

Another set of signals begins with giving or holding recognition of a country. The former acknowledges legitimacy and permanence; the latter signals disapproval or even a wish for downfall. Once relations are established, signals in more-or-less descending order of severity are breaking off diplomatic relations, expulsion of an ambassador, downgrading of relations (e.g., from ambassador to charge d'affairs), and ceremonial slights. All of these signals are, of course, reversible.

Although not in a negotiating context, there are several interesting examples using clothing as signals. Kemal Ataturk signalled his intention to secularize and westernize Turkey by forcing his people to abandon traditional Islamic garb, including the fez. Peter the Great did much the same 17th century Russia. Reversing this, Khomeini, Zia and Ghandi all adopted traditional garb to symbolize a turn *from* western values; Ghandi also adopted the spinning wheel as a symbol of national sufficiency (it remains on the Indian flag). Sun Yat Sen devised the "Mao jacket" to symbolize equality, modernity, and work. The communists later chose it to acknowledge their debt to Sun Yat Sen and to reaffirm his goals. Worn en masse by the typically large Chinese delegations, it conveys a grim remorseless determination that might influence bargaining climate.

45. SILENCE. Silence can emphasize a point, give the audience an opportunity to absorb a point or reflect on it, or simply regain attention. Silence is preferable to saying too much. For example, bargaining strength is lost by revealing how soon one needs to make a purchase, or that a particular product is the only one with the particular design feature meeting one's needs.

Opponents are expected to reply when a negotiator finishes a statement. If they do not, merely looking expectantly for more information, the negotiator often becomes uncomfortable and continues speaking, giving away more information than intended. A negotiator whose comments are answered by silence normally should wait in silence, without retracting, muttering, fidgeting or supplementing what has been said. But, if the silence is an opportunity to seize the initiative or if the opponent is confused, there is advantage in breaking the silence.

46. SPLIT THE DIFFERENCE. To split the difference is to agree to a settlement between the current proposals of each party. The implied split is halfway between the current positions. But a more aggressive negotiator can interpret an offer to split the difference as a concession by the opponent to the midpoint and seek to determine if further concessions can be gained. In doing so, it is important to drive home the point that half the difference already has been conceded by repeating your understanding of the opponents' new position, then rejecting it as unsatisfactory. Alternatively, you could say that you cannot afford a 50-50 split, then wait for the response. Or, you could suggest a split other than 50-50, such as 80-20 in your favor. In this case you should expect to haggle over it, perhaps ending at 60-40.

47. TAKE IT OR LEAVE IT. A very direct way to indicate to an opponent that the proposal being made at the moment represents the last possible concession (whether or not that is true) is to end by saying with at least some degree of anger " . . . and you can take it or leave it." This seldom does the bargaining climate any good, but is useful if it is likely to get a settlement.

There are variants that are not quite as blunt. One, already discussed, is "You'll have to do better than that." Even gentler, is telling the seller that you love their product or service but simply cannot afford the requested price, then to offer what you believe to be a barely acceptable price just above the sellers' deadlock price.

The variations on "take it or leave it" are intended to make sellers think they may lose an acceptable deal if they continue to push for maximum profits. But, sellers are not without recourse. The offered price can become a down payment with the balance paid in installments, or the seller can offer to meet the price if the buyer does not require delivery, can accept a delay in filling the order, can guarantee a large enough order to make such a discount feasible, can promise long-term or large-quantity orders, or can pay in full in advance. This tests how serious the buyers' budget limit is.

Another possibility is to suggest a lesser quality product or service (the standard instead of the deluxe model). This can be made more palatable if preceded by an offer of a careful review of the opponents' needs with a view toward finding a way of meeting them within their budget.

48. THREATS (or Ultimatums).   Threats and ultimatums suggest unpleasant consequences if a proposal is not accepted. The consequences can be ambiguous or clear, depending on the offerors' assessment of which will be most effective.

A threat interpreted as bluff regardless of how it was meant will be ignored and further concessions sought. If the threat was seriously intended the recipient may be in for a nasty surprise when negotiations are broken off and the threats carried out.

A threat taken seriously regardless of how it was meant leaves the recipient a choice between accepting the terms or suffering the consequences. The reaction to such a condition depends on several factors, most importantly whether the offer meets the opponents' negotiating objectives and whether the recipient can find a way to neutralize the threat. Some approaches that have worked have been transferring the negotiation to the next level of authority, responding as if the threat never had been received and getting agreement to "stop the clock" until agreement can be reached. The latter provides a face-saving way for all parties to ignore the threat.

A threat is most effective if made near opponents' deadlines or if coupled with an offer that falls between the opponents' realistic and deadlock positions. Early or frequent reliance on threats as a bargaining tool affects a negotiators bargaining reputation, which quickly deteriorates to that of "bully" or "boy who cries wolf." But, even this can be exploited. Before attacking Israel in 1972, Sadat carried out a series of bluffs, so that preparations for the real attack were seen as just another bluff.

49. TOUGHNESS. Tough negotiators are those who start with extreme positions, make small concessions and make them slowly. Generally, toughness pays off, but it may merely make opponents tough, increase the time required to reach agreement and detract from the bargaining climate.

Toughness can be overdone, and it can backfire in late delivery or late payment, poor quality or complaints, switching to the competition or taking advantage of any change in specifications that must be made. But erring in the opposite direction, that of offering unreciprocated concessions in hope of rapid progress, usually leads negotiators to conclude that their opponents are so desperate for agreement that patience alone will lead to an incredibly advantageous agreement. Russians are prone to the first, Americans to the second error.

Toughness may be an unwanted consequence of media interest in a negotiation. Negotiators may find it difficult to make face saving concessions if their early positions have been given undue publicity.

50. TIMING. With apologies to the Preacher, in every negotiation there is a time to speak and a time to listen, a time to resist and a time to give in, a time to question and a time to answer. Timing is one of the most subtle factors in a negotiation, developed slowly and only by experience.

The right move made too early or too late can be as ineffective as making the wrong move. The complexity of most negotiations, the number of tactics and their possible combinations and permutations insure that mistakes will be made.

SELECTED BIBLIOGRAPHY

BUSINESS

J. Auer and C. E. Harris. *Computer Contract Negotiations*. New York: Van Nostrand Reinhold, 1981.

J. Auer and C. E. Harris. *Major equipment Procurement*. New York: Van Nostrand Reinhold, 1983.

C. Barlow and G. Eisen. *Purchasing Negotiations*. Boston: CBI Publishing, 1983.

M. Bazerman & R. Lewicki, *Negotiating in Organizations*. Beverly Hills, CA: Sage, 1983.

M. Blaker, *Japanese International Negotiation*. New York: Columbia University, 1977.

D. Brandon and S. Segelstein. *Data Processing Contracts*. New York: Van Nostrand Reinhold, 1976.

L. Brown, *Managing Conflict at Organizational Interfaces*. Reading, MA: Addison-Wesley, 1983.

H. Calero & B. Oskam. *Negotiate the Deal You Want*. New York: Dodd, Mead & Company, 1983.

R. Contino. *Legal and Financial Aspects of Equipment Leasing Transactions*. Englewood Cliffs, NJ: Prentice-Hall, 1979.

J. Freund. *Anatomy of a Merger: Strategies and Techniques for Negotiating Corporate Acquisitions*. New York: Law Journal Seminars Press, 1975.

C. Harris, *Business Negotiating Power*. New York: Van Nostrand Reinhold, 1983.

J. Herz and C. Baller, eds. *Business Acquisitions*. New York: Practicing Law Institute, 1981 (2nd ed).

W. Hirsch, 1987?. The Contracts Managment Deskbook (Revised).

T. Hoffman. *How to Negotiate Successfully in Real Estate*. New York: Simon and Schuster, 1984.

T. Hopkins. *How to Master the Art of Selling*. New York: Warner, 1982.

D. Lax and J. Sebenius. *The Manager as Negotiator*. New York: The Free Press, 1986.

B. McVay, 1987. Getting Started in Federal Contracting. Woodbridge, VA: Panoptic Enterprises.

L. Mandell. *The Preparation of Commercial Agreements*. New York: Practicing Law Institute, 1978.

W. Messner. *Profitable Purchasing Management*. New York: Amacom, 1982.

B. Percelay and P. Arnold. *Packaging Your Home for Profit*. New York: Little, Brown, 1986.

INTERNATIONAL

E. Abel, *The Missile Crisis*. New York: Bantam, 1966.

D. Acheson, *Meetings at the Summit: a Study in Diplomatic Method*. Durham, NH: University of New Hampshire, 1958.

G. Allison, *Essence of Decision: Explaining the Cuban Missile Crisis*. Boston: Little, Brown and Company, 1971.

S. Bialer and M. Mandelbaum. *Gorbachev's Russia and American Foreign Policy*. Boulder, CO: Westview. 1988.

J. Burton. *Resolving Deep-rotted Conflict: A Handbook*. Lanham, MD: University Press of America. 1987.

W. Christopher, *American Hostages in Iran*. New Haven: Yale University Press, 1985.

R. Cohen, *The Art of Diplomatic Signalling*. White Plains, NY: Longmans, 1987.

J. Dedring, *Recent Advances in Peace and Conflict Research*. Beverly Hills, CA: Sage, 1976.

A. Eban, *The New Diplomacy*. New York: Random House, 1983.

F. Ikle, *How Nations Negotiate*. Millwood, NY: Krauss, 1964.

F. Ikle, *Every War Must End*. New York: Columbia University Press, 1971.

R. Kennedy, *Thirteen Days: A Memoir of the Cuban Missile Crisis*. New York: Norton, 1971.

H. Kissinger, *A World Restored: Castlereagh, Metternich and the Restoration of peace 1812-1822*. Boston: Hougton Mifflin, nd.

H. Kissinger, *White House Years*. Boston: Little, Brown and Company, 1979.

H. Kissinger, *Years of Turmoil*. Boston, Little, Brown and Company, 1982.

C. Mee, *The End of Order*. New York: Dutton, 1980.

P. Pillar, *Negotiating Peace: War Termination as a Bargaining Process*. Princeton: Princeton University Press, 1983.

P. Salinger, *America Held Hostage*. Garden City, NY: Doubleday, 1981.

R. Smoke, 1987. *Paths to Peace: Exploring the Feasibility of Sustainable Peace*. Boudler, CO: Westview.

J. Whelan, *Soviet Diplomacy and Negotiating Behavior*. Boulder, CO: Westview Press, 1983.

I. Zartman and M. Berman, *The Practical Negotiator*, New Haven: Yale University Press, 1982.

SOCIAL AND COMMUNITY

American Bar Association, *Alternative Means of Family Dispute Resolutions*. Washington, DC: author.

American Bar Association, *Family Law Quarterly,* 17, 4, Winter, 1984.

L. Bacow and M. Wheeler, *Environmental Dispute Resolution*. New York: Plenum, 1985.

R. Barker, *Not Here, But in Another Place*. New York: St. Martin's, 1980.

M. Berke & J. Grant, *Games Divorced People Play*. Englewood Cliffs, NJ: Prentice Hall, 1981.

G. Bermant, et. al. *The Ethics of Social Intervention*. Washington, Hemisphere, 1978.

F. Bienenfield, *Child Custody Mediation*, Palo Alto, CA: Science and Behavior.

G. Bingham. Resolving Environmental Disputes: A Decade of Experience. Washington, DC: The Conservation foundation. 1986.

W. Chalmers, *Racial Negotiations: Potentials and Limitations*. Ann Arbor: University of Michigan, 1974.

J. Coleman, *Community Conflict*. Glencoe, IL: The Free Press, 1957.

O. Coogler, *Structured Mediation in Divorce Settlement*. Lexington, MA: Lexington, Books, 1978.

R. Coulson, *Fighting Fair: Family Mediation Will Work for You*. New York: Macmillan, 1983.

P. Gulliver, *Disputes and Negotiations: A Cross-cultural Perspective*. New York: Academic Press, 1979.

J. Haynes, *Divorce Mediation: A Practical Guide for Counselors and Therapist*. New York: Springer, 1981.

J. Himes, *Conflict and Conflict Management*. Athens, GA: University of Georgia Press, 1980.

D. Kolb. *The Mediators*. Cambridge, MA: The MIT Press, 1983.

D. Maynard, *Inside Plea Bargaining: The Language of Negotiation*. New York: Plenum, 1985.

R. Paine. Dam a River, Dam a People?: Saami Livelihood and the Al Ta/Kautokeino Hydro-Electric Project. Cambridge, MA: Cultural Survival, Inc., 1982.

S. Ramos, *The Complete Book: Child Custody*. New York: G.P. Putnam's Sons, 1979.

I. Ricci, *Mom's House, Dad's House*. New York: Collier Books.

M. Robert, *Managing Conflict*. Austin, TX: Learning Concepts, 1982.

T. Sullivan: *Resolving Development Disputes Through Negotiations*. New York: Plenum, 1985.

L. Susskind and J. Cruikshank. Breaking the Impasse: Consensual Approaches to Resolving Public Disputes. New York: Basic Books. 1987.

L. Susskind. *Resolving Environmental Regulatory Disputes*. Cambridge, MA: Schenkman, 1984.

J. Van Fleet, *Power with People*. West Nyack, NY: Parker Publishing, 1972.

R. Walton, *Interpersonal Peacemaking: Confrontation and Third Party Consultation*. Reading, MA: Addison-Wesley, 1969.

C. Ware, *Sharing Parenthood After Divorce*. New York: The Viking Press, 1979.

R. Williams, *Mutual Accomodation: Ethnic Conflict and Cooperation*. Minneapolis: University of Minnesota Press, 1977.

SALARY

R. Bolles. *What Color is Your Parachute*. Berkeley: Ten Speed Press, 1976.

S. Chastain. *Winning the Salary Game: Salary Negotiation for Women*. New York: John Wiley & Sons, 1980.

F. Greenburger and T. Kiernan. *How to Ask for More and Get It*. New York: Doubleday, 1978.

R. Irish, *Go Hire Yourself an Employer*, New York: Anchor/Doubleday, 1973.

J. Tarrant. *How to Negotiate a Raise*. New York: Van Nostrand-Reinhold, 1976.

J. Tarrant. *Perks and Parachutes: Negotiating Your Executive Employment Contract*. New York: Simon & Schuster, 1985.

LABOR-MANAGEMENT

A. Bent & T. Reeves, *Collective Bargaining in the Public Sector*. Menlo Park, CA: Benjamin Cummings, 1978.

Bureau of National Affairs, Inc., *Grievance Guide*. Washington, DC: Author, 1978.

N. Chamberlain & J. Kuhn, *Collective Bargaining*. New York: McGraw-Hill, 1965.

R. Coulson, *The Termination Handbook*. New York: Free Press, 1981.

H. Davey, *Contemporary Collective Bargaining*. Englewood Cliffs, NJ: Prentice- Hall, 1977.

S. Heptonstall, *Making a Case*. Geneva: International Labor Office, 1979.

J. Kuhn, *Bargaining in Grievance Settlement*. New York: Columbia University Press, 1961.

C. Peck, *Cases and Materials on Negotiations*. Washington, DC: Bureau of National Affairs, 1980.

A. Sloane & F. Witney, *Labor Relations*. Englewood Cliffs, NJ: Prentice-Hall, 1977.

C. Stevens, *Strategy in Collective Bargaining Negotiation*. New York: McGraw-Hill, 1963.

L. Stessin & L. Smedresman, *The Encyclopedia of Collective Bargaining Contract Clauses*. New York: Business Research Publications Inc., 1980.

R. Walton and R. McKersie, *A Behavioral Theory of Labor Negotiations*. New York: McGraw-Hill, 1965.

A. Zack & R. Bloch, *Labor Agreement in Negotiation and Arbitration*. Washington, DC: Bureau of National Affairs, Inc., 1983.

TECHNIQUE AND THEORY

R. Andree, *The Art of Negotiation*. Lexington, MA: Heath Lexington Books, 1971.

S. Bachrach & E. Lawler, *Bargaining: Power, Tactics and Outcomes*. San Francisco: Jossey-Bass, 1981.

A. Benton, et. al., "Effects of extremity of offers and concession rate on the outcomes of bargaining." *Journal of Personality and Social Psychology*, 1972, 24, 73-83.

L. Coser, "Conflict: Social Aspects" in *International Encyclopedia of the Social Sciences, Vol 3*. New York: Macmillan, 1968.

L. Coser, *The Functions of Social Conflict*. Glencoe, IL: The Free Press, 1956.

J. Cross, *The Economics of Bargaining*. New York: Basic Books, 1969.

M. Deutsch, *The Resolution of Conflict*. New Haven: Yale, 1973.

J. England, "Mathematical models of two-party negotiations." *Behavioral Science, 18*, 1973.

R. Fisher and W. Ury, *Getting to Yes: Negotiating Agreement Without Giving In*. Boston: Hougton Mifflin, 1981.

N. Fraser and K. Hipel. *Conflict Analysis: Models and Resolutions*. New York: North-Holland, 1984.

J. Illich, *The Art and Skill of Successful Negotiation*. Englewood Cliffs, NJ: Prentice-Hall, 1973.

J. Illich and B. Jones, *Successful Negotiating Skills for Women*. New York: Playboy, 1981.

C. Karrass, *Give & Take: the Complete guide to Negotiating Strategies and Tactics*: New York: Thomas Y. Crowell, 1974.

C. Karrass, *The Negotiating Game*. Cleveland, OH: World, 1970.

R & R. Likert, *New Ways of Managing Conflict*. New York: McGraw-Hill, 1976.

A. Maslow (*Motivation and Personality*, New York: Harper & Row, 1954).

G. Nierenberg, *Fundamentals of Negotiating*. New York: Hawthorn, 1973.

D. Pruitt, *Negotiation Behavior*. New York: Academic Press, 1981.

H. Raiffa, *Art and Science of Negotiation*. Cambridge, MA: Harvard University Press, 1982.

M. Roloff, *Interpersonal Communication*. Beverly Hills, CA: Sage, 1981.

M. Roloff & G. Miller, Editors, *Persuasion*. Beverly Hills, CA: Sage, 1980.

J. Rubin and B. Brown, *The Social Psychology of Bargaining and Negotiation*. New York: Academic Press, 1975.

J. Schellenberg, *Science of Conflict*. New York: Oxford University Press, 1982.

B. Scott, *Negotiating*. New York: John Wiley & Sons, 1981.

T. Schelling, *The Strategy of Conflict*. Cambridge, MA: Harvard University Press, 1962.

G. Shure, "The effectiveness of pacifist strategies in bargaining games." *The Journal of Conflict Resolution, 9, 1965.*

S. Siegel and L. Fouraker, *Bargaining and Decision Making*. New York: McGraw-Hill, 1960.

D. Sparks, *The Dynamics of Effective Negotiation*. Houston: Gulf Publications, 1982.

A. Strauss, *Negotiations: Varieties, Contexts, Processes and Social Order*. San Francisco: Jossey-Bass, 1978.

V. Taylor, *The Art of Argument*. Metuchen, NJ: Scarecrow Press, 1971.

P. Wehr, *Conflict Regulation*. Boulder, CO: Westview Press, 1979.

O. Young, *Bargaining: Formal Theories of Negotiation*. Urbana: University of Illinois, 1975.

FICTION

R. Aron, *Paix et guerre entre les nations*. Paris: Calman-Levy, 1962.

M. Martin, *The Final Conclave*. New York: Stein and Day, 1978.

F. Walder, *The Negotiators*. McDowell, Obolensky, 1959.

RELATED TOPICS AND SPECIAL REFERENCES

J. Berke. *Twenty Questions for the Writer*. San Diego: Harcourt Brace Jovanovich, 1985 (4th. ed).

N. Capaldi, *The Art of Deception*, New York: Donald W. Brown, 1971.

D. Fisher, *Historians' Fallacies*. New York: Harper (Colophon Books). 1970.

J. Katzer, et. al., *Evaluating Information*. New York: Addison-Wesley, 1982.

J. Romer. *Ancient Lives*. New York: Holt, Rinehart and Winston, 1984.

INDEX

BASIC NEGOTIATING TACTICS

David Churchman

Behavioral Science Graduate Program
California State University, Dominguez Hills

Los Angeles

Published by: David Churchman
                  P. O. Box 43784
                  Los Angeles, CA 90043

Printed by: Dickerson Printing
                  Tucson, AZ 85712

Manufactured in the United States of America